Geoffrey Patterson

ALL ABOUT BREAD

ANDRE DEUTSCH

The author acknowledges with gratitude the help received from the following in the preparation of this book: Mike Dunn and Bernard Boyd, The Wheatsheaf Bakery, Harleston, Norfolk; Dan Keating, Fressingfield, Suffolk; George Gordon and John Wieghtman, Tooks Bakery, Ipswich, Suffolk; 'Cookie', Brockdish Bakery, Norfolk; The Suffolk Hovis Group; The Flour Advisory Bureau; Monsieur Orenga, Boulangerie de Pourcieux and Monsieur Lafite, Boulangerie de Grignoles.

First published in 1984 by
André Deutsch Limited
105 Great Russell Street London WC1

Printed and bound in Belgium by Proost, Turnhout.
Filmset in Erhardt by Filmtype Services Limited, Scarborough, North Yorkshire.

ISBN 233 97635 5

Bread is one of man's oldest foods, so old that we do not know exactly when it was first made.

What we do know is that bread-making came to Europe from the ancient civilisations of Asia and Egypt, and that the seeds of grains have been eaten ever since some primitive people somewhere discovered that the store of grains they uncovered in an ants' nest could be ground between two flat stones into flour.

There are many kinds of grain and over the centuries people have cultivated those most suited to their own climate. In temperate climates the most common cereals are wheat, barley, rye, oats and maize. Wheat, of which there are over 30,000 varieties, is the favourite cereal from which to grind bread flour.

Wheat grows best in good heavy soil in a temperate climate. It gives fine crops and the flour makes firm, satisfying bread. Wheat flour is often mixed with other flours for bread-making.

Barley will grow in poorer soil than wheat. The flour alone makes a bread too sweet for most tastes.

Rye is grown widely in Russia and Scandinavia. Bread made from its dark flour has a nutty flavour. A mixture of rye and wheat was the staple bread flour in Britain in the middle ages.

Wheat

Rye

Barley

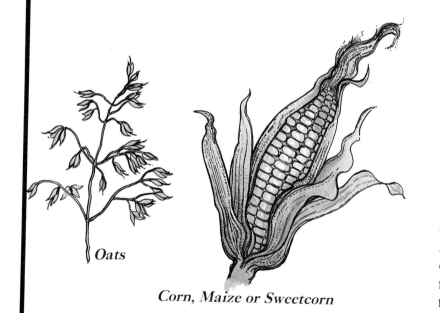

Oats

Corn, Maize or Sweetcorn

Oats grow well in climates which are wetter and colder than those which other grains prefer. The sweet flour makes a heavy rather moist bread. It is commonly used for making oatcakes.

Corn, Maize or Sweetcorn. In many places the word corn is used to describe all cereal grains, but Americans use the word to describe the full grained ear of the maize plant from which the North American Indians made bread. Sweetcorn ears are either eaten as a vegetable, fed to cattle or ground into flour. Corn meal makes a crumbly bread, so wheat flour is often mixed with it.

The process of grinding grain to make flour is called milling. Wholemeal flour is made from the whole grain, white flour is made from the central section of the grain only. The outer case or bran and the germ or embryo are not used.

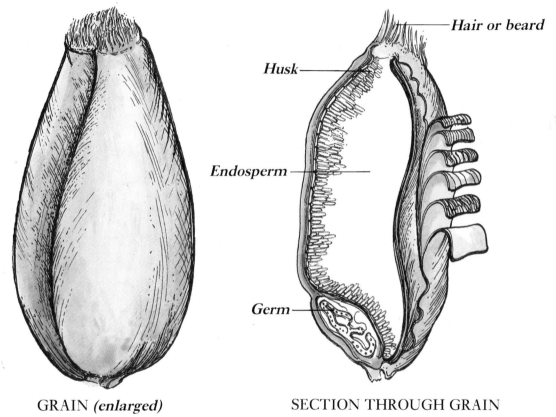

GRAIN *(actual size)*

GRAIN *(enlarged)*

SECTION THROUGH GRAIN

Hair or beard

Husk

Endosperm

Germ

Endosperm. The main part of the grain from which the flour is made. The food reserve on which the young plant lives.

Husk. The outer skins of the grain.

Germ. The part from which the new plant grows.

The first attempts people made to mill grain were very primitive. In the Stone and Iron Ages, for instance, seeds were not ground but crushed with a pestle in a mortar. The resulting flour was coarse and bitty. When people first started to grind corn they put the seed on a long, flat 'sloping' stone, and rubbed another smaller stone up and down over it. The meal produced was still coarse, but more evenly ground.

Copper, bronze and iron were first produced between three and one thousand years BC. As well as simple weapons and ornaments, basic cooking utensils were made, perhaps like this iron 'griddle' or plate for baking on.

A tool called a 'quern' was developed in the Far East and Egypt which really ground the grain, rather than just crushing it. A circular stone with a hole in it and a pole attached was placed flat on top of a larger circular stone. The top stone was turned with the pole, and the grain, poured in through the hole, worked its way between the stones where it was ground to flour. Turning the handle was slow, heavy work, but the flour was good.

A small quern. The wooden handle turns the whole of the hollowed out top stone.

The Romans developed the method of grinding grain between two stones by designing huge machines which could turn out enough flour for it to be sold at a profit. They used slaves to turn the upper stone and fed them on hard coarse bread called 'cibarus' which was made from the husks of the grain. They were first ground, then sifted through a coarsely woven bag of linen or rushes and mixed with water.

The Romans made bread on a massive scale. This is a typical bake house in Rome. Daily ovens like these would produce bread for 20,000 people using 25,000 kg or 50,000 lb of flour.

The Romans used yeast to make the bread rise. Yeast is a living fungus, and looks rather like soft cheese. When water (and sugar for it to feed on) are added, and the mixture is warmed, the yeast begins to release tiny bubbles of gas, which work in the dough. Baked bread 'leavened' with yeast is light and soft to eat.

Watermills were in use before the birth of Christ. Antipater, a poet from Thessalonica, mentions a watermill in the year 85 BC: another reference in 65 BC is to a mill at Pontus. Both these mills were in Asia Minor.

Early mills like this one had horizontal wheels mounted on vertical shafts which drove the upper or runner stone. This is a very primitive mill and the wheel is turned by water from a stream channelled into a trough. Horizontal mills like this are called 'Norse mills' and are used in poor rural areas. They can still be found in use today in Europe and Asia.

The Domesday Book of 1086 lists 5624 mills in England.

'Tirl' wheel

CUT AWAY SECTION

Windmills came after watermills and are mentioned in records in Normandy and Provence in France in 1180, in Suffolk, England in 1185 and in Syria in 1190. Very early windmills might have looked like this. The sails were covered with stretched cloth, and all the arms braced to a bowsprit projecting from the wind shaft.

Windmills similar to this can be found today in Greece and Spain.

Windmills, watermills and even the very early hand-mills all work on the same principle which has changed little over the centuries.

The sails of the windmill were built on long poles so that the sails would be exposed to the wind as much as possible. Either the whole mill, like this one which was moved by revolving the mill with the tailpole, or just the top half revolved, so the sails could be set facing into the wind. The two grinding stones were used in both wind and watermills.

The sails, turned by the wind or the wheel pushed round and round by water, rotated the main drive wheel which was geared so as to turn the top stone, or runner, against the stationary bottom stone – or bedstone, as it was called.

Wind and water mills had a tremendous influence on the development of farming, for they meant farmers could grow large grain crops, knowing wind and water would always be available to provide the power they needed for grinding the grain into flour.

To build these corn mills was an expensive business so it was the lord of the manor, the church or the crown who built them. Payment was made in kind and was known as toll, usually one sixteenth of the grain brought to be ground.

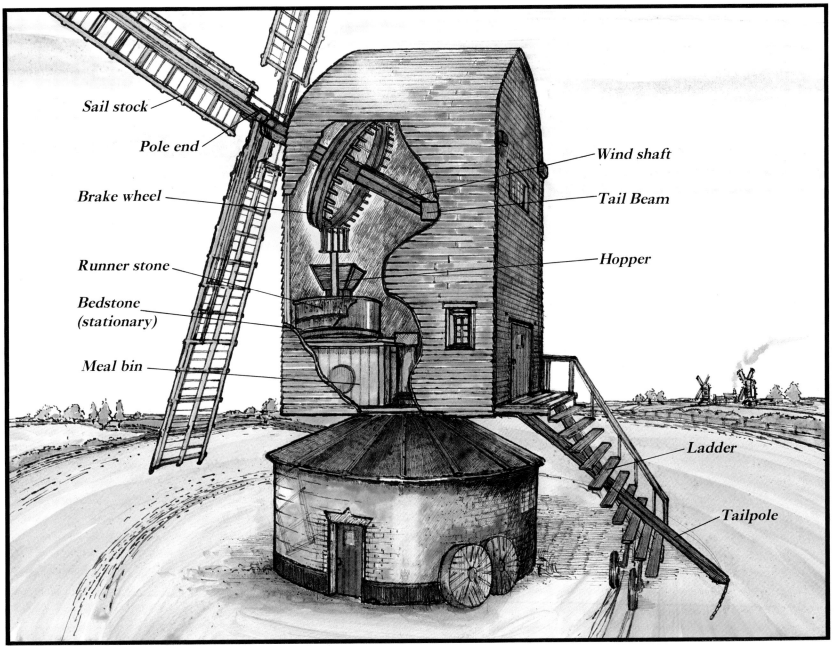

Sail stock

Pole end

Brake wheel

Runner stone

Bedstone
(stationary)

Meal bin

Wind shaft

Tail Beam

Hopper

Ladder

Tailpole

13

The circular grinding stones were usually made from Derbyshire Peak or French Burr. The Derbyshire millstones were quarried in one piece, about 1.0 to 1.5 metres (3′ 6″–5′) in diameter and holed in the centre. French Burr stones were usually quarried in sections, cemented together and held by iron hoops.

Stones are used in pairs – the bedstone is stationary and the runner stone turns above it. The stones are covered by a wooden casing called a vat or tun. The grain is fed from the hopper first into a wooden trough called the 'shoe' and then into the eye of the stone. The surface of the stone between the furrows is called

the 'land'. Little marks called 'cracks' or 'snecks' are made in it (about sixteen to the inch) to give maximum grinding power.

Long grooves called furrows spread the grain over the grinding surfaces and ventilate the stones to keep them cool.

Both stones need constant care to keep them sharp. Some flour is still stone-ground today and the man whose job it is to keep the grooves well sharpened is a skilled craftsman. He uses special tools for the grooving, which must always be done by hand.

Furrow

Cracking between furrows

In the Middle Ages food was often eaten off squares of coarse wholemeal bread called trenchers. When the meal was finished the trenchers, still soaked in gravy or cream, would be given to the poor to eat.

This is how the tradition grew up that wholemeal bread was only for the poor while the rich could afford refined white bread. Nowadays more and more people eat wholemeal bread, knowing it to be better food.

The word trencherman, meaning someone with a good appetite, derives from the trencher.

Buying bread ready baked from a bakery is a comparatively new idea. For centuries, whether you lived in the town or the country, you baked your bread at home in a specially built oven.

The faggot oven, as it was called, was brick built and often domed. It was fuelled with faggots – often apple wood which smelled sweet and gave off a good heat.

The dough was placed directly into the pre-heated rear of the oven. The fire or smoke-duct of the faggot oven was connected through the kitchen fireplace to the main chimney.

In Victorian times the faggot oven was replaced by a tin oven, called a Dutch oven, built into the kitchen range.

The brick built crown oven was the one most favoured by town bakers in the nineteenth century. The oven itself was narrow and low ceilinged, a good shape because it prevented too much moisture from evaporating from the bread. It was difficult to clean, however, and bakers used a long pole with a rag wrapped round the end to reach the furthest corners. They called it a scuffle pole.

The dough, a mixture of flour, salt, fat, yeast and water, was put in a warm 'proving' hole below the firebox to rise before being transferred to the oven for baking. Sometimes, if the bakery itself was warm enough, the dough was left to rise on shelves near the oven. This oven is fired by wood.

Main oven

Proving oven

17

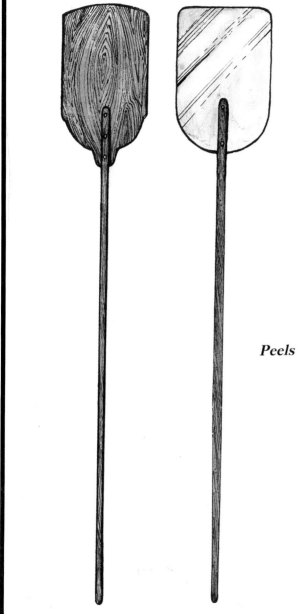

Peels

Dough bin scraper

Dough cutter

Commercial bakers need special tools to help them in their daily work.

One of the most used is the peel. This paddle-like tool was about 2.4 metres long, with the metal or wooden spade on the end of the wooden handle. It was used for setting in the dough and removing the baked bread later. The metal ended one was usually used for this because the thin edge was easy to slide under the cooked bread.

The dough bin scraper was used for scraping out the dough-bin and cleaning the kneading surfaces.

The dough cutter, a deep, sharp metal blade fixed to a wooden handle was used to cut dough into loaves.

Nineteenth century commercial bakers baked bread using the same methods as the housewife in a domestic kitchen, only on a larger scale. This baker is kneading the dough into loaves after first mixing the ingredients in the wooden trough, or dough bin.

The yeast bucket is set near the oven, where the warmth will activate the mixture of yeast, sugar and water, making it ready to be added to the next batch of flour.

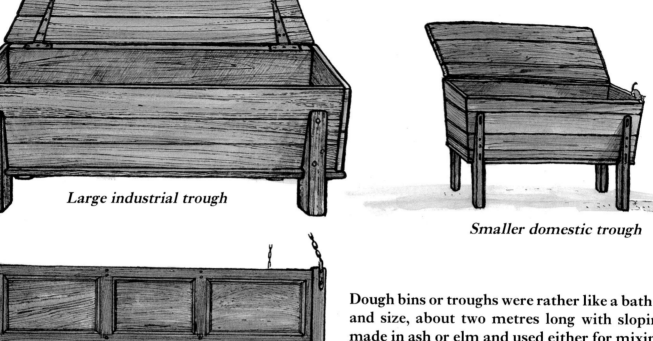

Large industrial trough

Smaller domestic trough

Cradle

Crock

Dough bins or troughs were rather like a bath in shape and size, about two metres long with sloping sides, made in ash or elm and used either for mixing dough or for storage.

Keeping bread fresh and out of the way of mice was always a problem. The great cradle (centre left) can be seen in the kitchen of St. Fagan's Castle in Wales. It was raised and lowered on ropes. The open grid at the bottom kept air circulating round the bread to stop it going mouldy.

The earthenware crock (bottom left) is another example of a container used to keep bread fresh and cool.

Damper

Hot water tank

Firebox

Ashbox

This is a coal fired oven built in 1933. The oven door, proving hole, firebox and ash box are all cast iron. The coal was loaded into the firebox and the heat it raised in the oven was controlled by the draught in the chimney which was controlled by a damper. One hundred weight of coal was needed to heat the brick built oven. First the oven would be loaded with about 200 loaves, a job that took some ten minutes. As the oven cooled off scones, buns and cakes would be baked. The oven shown here is still being used in Norfolk, but most small bakeries now use oil or gas fired ovens.

Strapped tins

Today ovens are gas or oil fired. This drawing shows a gas fired 'Reel' oven. It has six rotating shelves with the gas burner at the bottom. It can bake one hundred and twenty loaves in forty five minutes at 450 degrees F., and as the shelves rotate the bread is baked evenly.

The dough is put in tins fixed together in threes or fours, called strapped tins. They are first lined with silicon paper to stop the dough sticking. This type of oven is also very good for baking cakes and pastries.

This is a moulding machine which replaces the job of kneading the dough by hand. They are found in small bakeries. The right amount of freshly mixed dough is put in the machine, where it is gently kneaded by a series of moving belts and comes out ready to rise, before being cooked in the oven. It can produce a variety of sizes and shape of loaves. Machines exist now for doing all the jobs that were once done by hand, although many bakers believe that hand-made bread is best.

Today, dough is seldom mixed by hand; instead giant motorised mixing bowls do the job, this one can mix 112 lbs of flour together with the fat, salt, yeast and water. Some more complicated mixers heat the dough as they mix it to save time.

Nowadays, so much bread is eaten daily that it has to be made in huge quantities in factories called plant bakeries. Everything is done by machines. This is a typical plant oven producing 3,600 loaves an hour. The dough is automatically mixed and weighed and placed in grease-sprayed tins ready for baking. The baked bread is removed by hand from the oven, then the bread is sucked out of the tins by machine and fast cooled in an hour and a half. A metal detector scans the bread to make sure no pieces of metal from the machinery have fallen into it, then it is sliced, wrapped and loaded on to waiting vans for delivery.

Most people now buy their bread from the local baker or in supermarkets and grocers. But not so very long ago it was usual for the baker to deliver bread to his customers. The roundsman stocked his wicker basket up with loaves of all shapes and sizes and took it to the door. The customer paid for bread at the end of the week, giving the money to the roundsman. The horse became so used to the journey that he would pull the van from one door to the next, just on hearing a shout from the roundsman.

VICTORIA BAKERY
C. BYFORD.
7, LOWGATE STREET.
- EYE - SUFFOLK -

THE SEARCH FOR WHITE BREAD

Flour ground naturally from a whole grain is brown, nourishing and helpful to the digestion, but nevertheless, white flour has long been thought to make a loaf that is better to look at and pleasanter to eat, so people have gone to extraordinary lengths to make brown flour white.

Flour is sifted to separate the centre of the grains' white powder from the outer skins called bran. In the eighteenth century some bakers began to add other strange whitening ingredients such as ground up dried bones, wood ash, chalk, lime and even white lead, which is poisonous. They added alum to bleach the flour but this had such a constipating effect that bakers had to add the resin from the ground roots of a plant from Mexico called Jalap to put this right! By 1829 such bread was so impure that 'A Lady' published a book entitled 'A new system of Domestic Cooking' which warned readers against these whitening substances in bread, and told them how to detect them. This was a long time ago. Nowadays strict regulations control the quality and enrichment of flour used in bread-making.

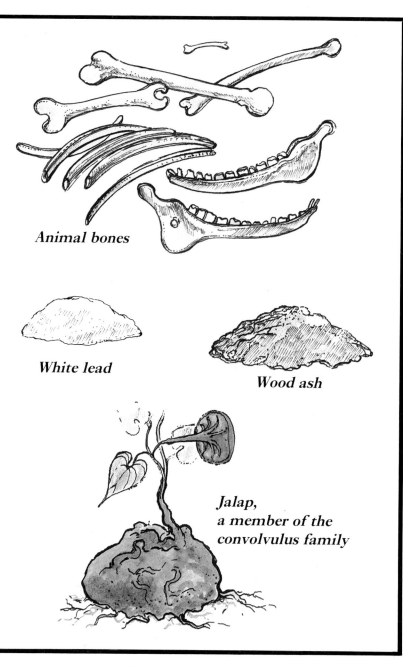

Animal bones

White lead

Wood ash

*Jalap,
a member of the
convolvulus family*

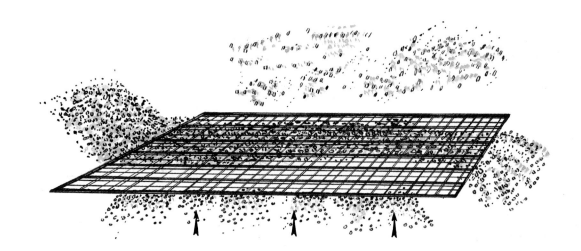

Air

Impurities, such as grit and unwanted parts of mixed grains, are removed by sieving and blowing the lighter parts away.

To produce enough flour to make a loaf you need about two square metres of land. Most people eat some 70 kgs of flour a year. Steel roller mills, now used all over the world but originally designed in Hungary, make it possible to grind flour to a chosen degree of fineness. By setting the rollers as you want them you can have either fine white flour made almost entirely from the starchy endosperm of the grain (see P.6), or you can have a coarser brown flour which uses the husk as well as the endosperm. Unless the flour is completely wholemeal then a certain amount of the goodness is bound to be lost during the milling. This is replaced by adding vitamins such as B 1.

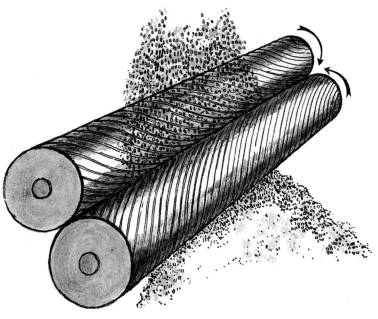

One of the most popular ways of eating bread is as a sandwich. The sandwich is named after John Montague, 4th Earl of Sandwich, who lived from 1718–1792. He had a distinguished political career and was First Lord of the Admiralty, but he also enjoyed gambling and the sandwich got its name in 1762, when he spent twenty four hours at a gaming table, never stopping to take food other than pieces of meat which were brought to him between two slices of bread.

In many countries, particularly France, people consider it important to buy their bread freshly baked each day, if possible twice a day. The baguette, or French stick, is one of the favourite loaves in France.

It is usually baked in the French baker's own shop or 'Boulangerie', which is the first shop to open and the last to shut each day.

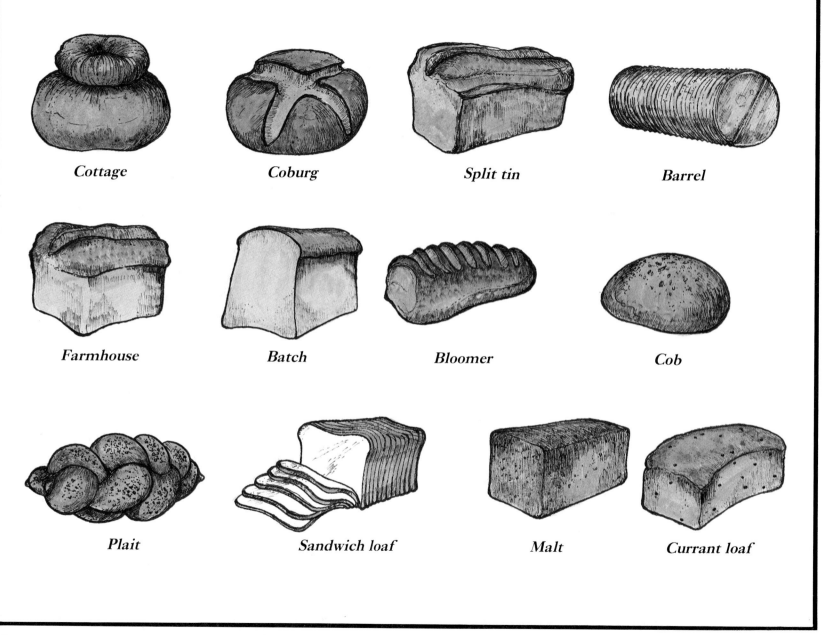

Cottage

Coburg

Split tin

Barrel

Farmhouse

Batch

Bloomer

Cob

Plait

Sandwich loaf

Malt

Currant loaf

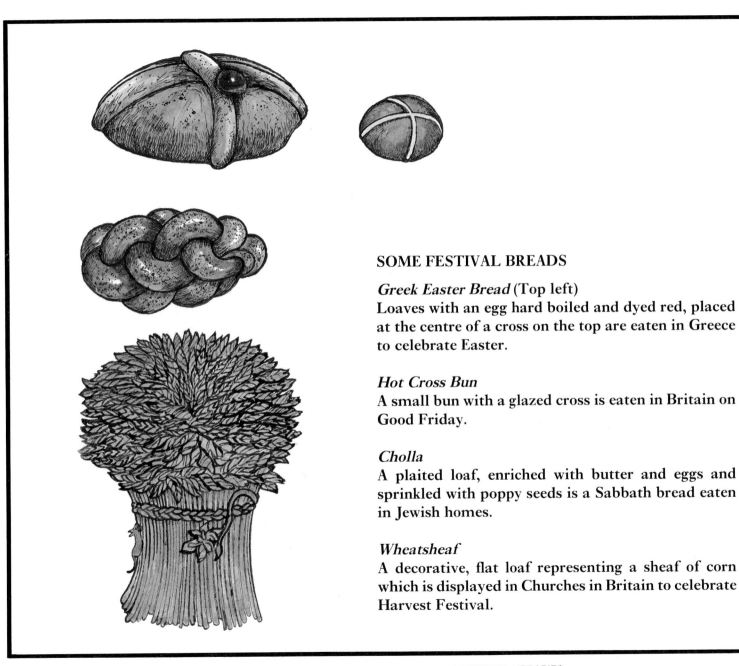

SOME FESTIVAL BREADS

Greek Easter Bread (Top left)
Loaves with an egg hard boiled and dyed red, placed at the centre of a cross on the top are eaten in Greece to celebrate Easter.

Hot Cross Bun
A small bun with a glazed cross is eaten in Britain on Good Friday.

Cholla
A plaited loaf, enriched with butter and eggs and sprinkled with poppy seeds is a Sabbath bread eaten in Jewish homes.

Wheatsheaf
A decorative, flat loaf representing a sheaf of corn which is displayed in Churches in Britain to celebrate Harvest Festival.

INDEX

PRINTED IN BELGIUM BY

INTERNATIONAL BOOK PRODUCTION